Dare To Be Great, Ms. Caucus

Dare To Be Great, Ms. Caucus

a *Doonesbury* book by G.B. Trudeau

Holt, Rinehart and Winston
New York

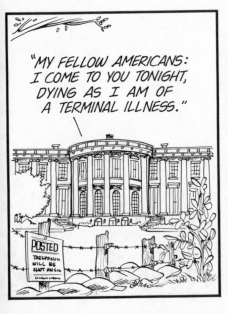

To: Photo Editor
From: Roland Burton Hedley, Jr.

This is Zonker Harris, 19, member of Walden.

Walden Commune — located about ½ mile from campus..

This is the backyard marijuana plant, which Zonker claims yields the highest grade grass in New England!

ROLAND, THAT'S A LILAC BUSH!

IT IS?..

OH, LACEY! — REMEMBER WHEN WE GRADUATED, I WENT RIGHT OFF AND GOT THAT JOB CLERKING IN BOSTON?

YES, AND I STAYED ON AND GOT MY LAW DEGREE, AND LATER JOINED A PRESTIGIOUS NEW YORK FIRM..

.. AND THEN WHEN I WAS LAID OFF, YOU SUPPORTED ME FOR THIRTY YEARS, SO I COULD PURSUE MY HOBBY, ORNITHOLOGY.

BUT YOU KEPT UP YOUR PART OF THE BARGAIN, DICK — YOU TOOK CARE OF THE HOUSE. AND IT WAS ALWAYS NEAT AS A PIN!

OH, LACEY... MARRY ME!

DICK, DICK — THAT'S CHAMPAGNE SPEAKING, NOT LOVE.

YOU'RE RIGHT... BUT LET US BE GAY!

YES, LET'S, DEAR HEART! REMEMBER THE FALL OF '29?

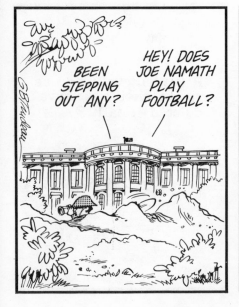

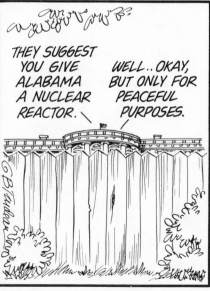